D1492561

HOW DOES IT FLY?

The Science of Flight

Library of Congress Cataloging-in-Publication Data

Rees, Peter.
  How does it fly? : the science of flight / by Peter Rees.
      p. cm. -- (Shockwave)
  Includes index.
  ISBN-10: 0-531-17587-1 (lib. bdg.)
  ISBN-13: 978-0-531-17587-3 (lib. bdg.)
  ISBN-10: 0-531-18816-7 (pbk.)
  ISBN-13: 978-0-531-18816-3 (pbk.)

  1. Aeronautics--Juvenile literature. 2. Flight--Juvenile literature.
I. Title. II. Series.

  TL547.R44 2007
  629.13--dc22

2007016732

Published in 2008 by Children's Press, an imprint of Scholastic Inc.,
557 Broadway, New York, New York 10012
www.scholastic.com

SCHOLASTIC, CHILDREN'S PRESS, and associated logos are trademarks
and/or registered trademarks of Scholastic Inc.

08 09 10 11 12 13 14 15 16 17
10 9 8 7 6 5 4 3 2 1

Printed in China through Colorcraft Ltd., Hong Kong

Author: Peter Rees
Educational Consultant: Ian Morrison
Editor: Nerida Frost
Designer: Pirzad Rustomjee
Illustration: Spike Wademan (pp. 28–29)
Photo Researcher: Jamshed Mistry

Photographs by: AAP Image/AP/Elaine Thompson (Dreamlifter pp. 30–31; **Arne V. Petersen,
Copenhagen Airports A/S** (removing ice, p. 26; **BAA Aviation Photo Library/www.baa.com/
photolibrary** (pp. 10–11; ground controller, pp. 12–13; preflight check, p. 14; preflight wheel
check, p. 19; landing, refueling, pp. 22–23; fire drill, p. 24; **Courtesy of Drs. B. Th. Horsmans/
www.horsmans.com** (horses, p. 31); **Digital Vision** (pilot at controls, pp. 14–15); **Getty Images**
(tug and plane, p. 13); **Jennifer and Brian Lupton** (teenagers, pp. 32–33); **NASA/©Italian Space
Agency** (nose-flap opening, p. 31); **Photolibrary** (cover; air-traffic control tower, p. 12; Piper
Cherokees, p. 15; emergency practice, pp. 16–17; boy, p. 18; aircraft maintenance, Boeing 747
engine check, pp. 20–21); **Reuters** (p. 7; flight simulator, p. 17); **Rex Features** (sniffer dog,
p. 10; low-flying plane, pp. 32–33); **Tranz: Corbis** (p. 3; pp. 8–9; takeoff, pp. 18–19; takeoff,
p. 21; wing flap, p. 22; lightning strike, black box, pp. 26–27; p. 29); **www.airbus.com**
(evacuation, pp. 24–25)

The publisher would like to thank Captain Ian Murray (retired British Airways pilot)
for his expert advice, and Arne Peterson for the photo of ice being removed on page 26.

All other illustrations and photographs © Weldon Owen Education Inc.

SHOCKWAVE
SCIENCE

HOW DOES IT FLY?

The Science of Flight

Peter Rees

children's press®

An imprint of Scholastic Inc.
NEW YORK • TORONTO • LONDON • AUCKLAND • SYDNEY
MEXICO CITY • NEW DELHI • HONG KONG
DANBURY, CONNECTICUT

CHECK THESE OUT!

SHOCKER

Stuff to Shock,
Surprise, and
Amaze You

Quick Recaps
and Notable
Notes

Word Stunners
and Other Oddities

The Heads-Up
on Expert Reading

Links to More
Information

CONTENTS

HIGH-POWERED WORDS   6

GET ON THE WAVELENGTH   8

Checking In   10

Welcome Aboard!   12

In the Cockpit   14

Flight Simulator   16

Taking Off   18

In the Air   20

Finding the Way   22

Safety in the Sky   24

Lucky Escapes   28

Cargo Carriers   30

AFTERSHOCKS   32

GLOSSARY   34

FIND OUT MORE   35

INDEX   36

ABOUT THE AUTHOR   36

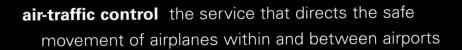
air-traffic control the service that directs the safe
movement of airplanes within and between airports

autopilot an airplane electronic control system
that automatically maintains a flight path

aviation (*ay vee AY shuhn*) the science of building
and flying aircraft

fuselage (*FYOO suh lahj*) the main body of the airplane
that holds the crew, passengers, luggage, and cargo

navigation (*nav uh GAY shuhn*) finding the way when
traveling, often with the help of maps, compasses,
or the stars

radar (*RAY dar*) a device that locates objects by reflecting
radio waves off them and receiving the reflected waves

taxi to move slowly on the ground or on the surface of
the water in an airplane before takeoff or after landing

. . . .

For additional vocabulary, see Glossary on page 34.

The word *radar* is an acronym,
a word made up of the beginning
letters of other words. Radar stands
for *radio detection and ranging*.

Airports are full of activity. The minute you step inside, you can feel the excitement. An average airport is like a town unto itself. You will find everything – from restaurants and stores to banks and gyms. Thousands of people work in an airport. There are cleaners and cooks, safety crews and search-dog handlers. It takes a community nearly the size of a small town to keep an airport running smoothly!

Have you ever wondered what happens to your luggage after check-in, or how an **autopilot** works? This book answers these questions and more. So welcome aboard. Enjoy your flight. By the end of your journey, you will know much more about flying in the twenty-first century.

WORLD'S BUSIEST AIRPORTS

Airport	Passenger Departures/Arrivals Per Year
Hartsfield International, Atlanta	83,606,583
O'Hare International, Chicago	75,533,822
Heathrow, London	67,344,054
Haneda, Tokyo	62,291,405
Los Angeles International	60,688,609
Dallas/Fort Worth International	59,412,217
Charles de Gaulle, Paris	51,260,363
Frankfurt, Germany	51,098,271
Schiphol, Amsterdam	42,541,180
Denver International	42,393,766

CHECKING IN

What happens to luggage?

The tags the check-in agent sticks on the bags store all information about flights and destinations in a bar code. After check-in, the bags pass through scanners that read the tags and send the bags on their journey along a system of conveyors and automated railways. The bags are x-rayed and checked by search dogs for items such as illegal drugs or explosives.

Hundreds of computers control the junctions and switches on the railway, as well as keep track of every bag on its journey. At the end, the bags arrive at a sorting station, where baggage handlers load them onto carts and take them to the cargo hold of the correct airplane.

I like the question/answer format. The questions are ones I would really ask. The answers explain some pretty complex ideas, as well as providing lots of other interesting information.

Airport search dog at work

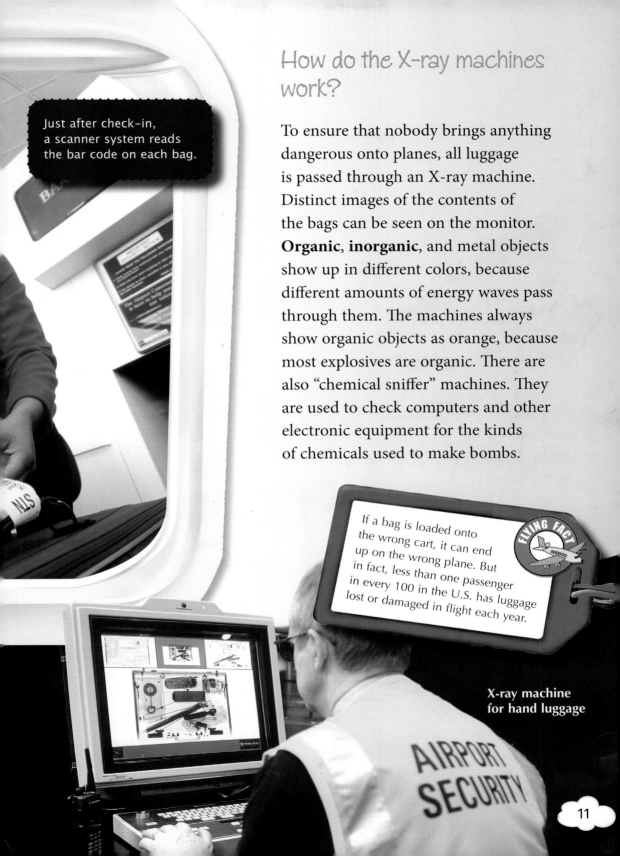

How do the X-ray machines work?

To ensure that nobody brings anything dangerous onto planes, all luggage is passed through an X-ray machine. Distinct images of the contents of the bags can be seen on the monitor. **Organic**, **inorganic**, and metal objects show up in different colors, because different amounts of energy waves pass through them. The machines always show organic objects as orange, because most explosives are organic. There are also "chemical sniffer" machines. They are used to check computers and other electronic equipment for the kinds of chemicals used to make bombs.

FLYING FACT

If a bag is loaded onto the wrong cart, it can end up on the wrong plane. But in fact, less than one passenger in every 100 in the U.S. has luggage lost or damaged in flight each year.

X-ray machine for hand luggage

WELCOME ABOARD!

What's that tower beside the runway?

In the **air-traffic control** tower, air-traffic controllers direct airplanes in the same way that police officers direct road traffic. However, air-traffic controllers use **radar** and computers for the job. Different controllers are responsible for each stage of the flight.

Ground controllers guide airplanes as they **taxi** to and from the runway. Tower controllers take over to direct takeoffs and landings. Other controllers take charge once the airplanes are in flight. As a plane travels, it is handed from one air-traffic control center to another.

Air-traffic control tower

What are those people on the runway doing?

Most of those people are ground crew. They are responsible for checking, loading, and refueling the airplanes. You might even see a pilot walking around an airplane. The preflight checks include a thorough inspection of the outside of the aircraft by one of the pilots.

The people waving orange paddles are called marshalers. Their job is to guide airplanes to the gates after they have landed. Other ground crew drive low, flat trucks, called tugs, which push or pull the airplanes into position.

Taking Control
- In the air: air-traffic controllers
- On the runway: ground controllers
- To and from gates: marshalers

Tug

IN THE COCKPIT

What does the pilot do?

Every airplane has two pilots in case one pilot becomes sick and can't fly. The captain sits in the left seat of the cockpit and is in charge of the flight. The first officer, also known as the copilot, sits on the right. He or she assists with preflight checks and takes over flying about half the time. There is also a computer autopilot. Autopilots are used mainly to give the pilots a rest during long flights. The autopilots use computers and sensors on the plane to keep the airplane on course and fuel **consumption** low. Modern autopilots can even help land the airplane in thick fog. However, the pilots still do the bulk of the work during takeoff and landing.

Pilot was a word long before there were any airplanes! Centuries before the first person steered a plane, a pilot was a person who steered a ship.

While one of the pilots carries out an outside check of the aircraft, the other boards the plane to do the flight deck preflight checks.

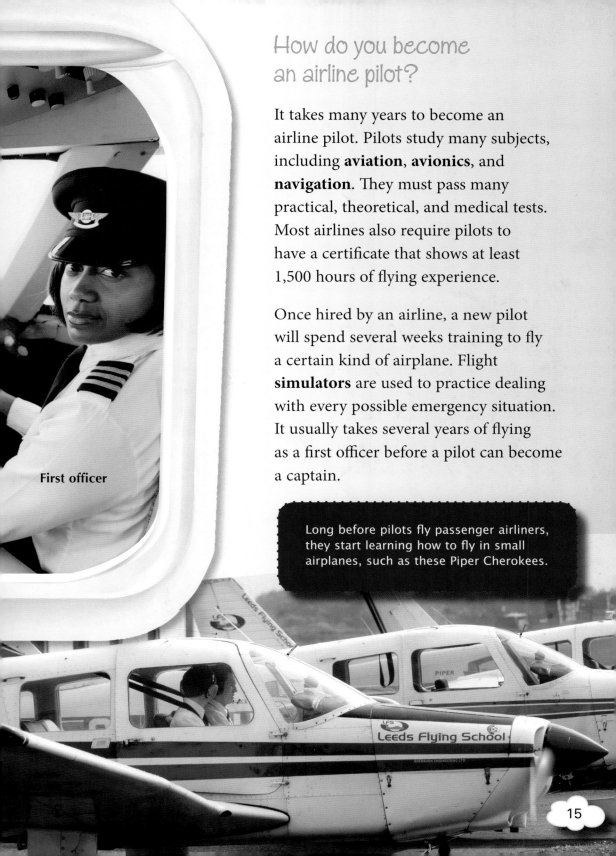

How do you become an airline pilot?

It takes many years to become an airline pilot. Pilots study many subjects, including **aviation**, **avionics**, and **navigation**. They must pass many practical, theoretical, and medical tests. Most airlines also require pilots to have a certificate that shows at least 1,500 hours of flying experience.

Once hired by an airline, a new pilot will spend several weeks training to fly a certain kind of airplane. Flight **simulators** are used to practice dealing with every possible emergency situation. It usually takes several years of flying as a first officer before a pilot can become a captain.

First officer

Long before pilots fly passenger airliners, they start learning how to fly in small airplanes, such as these Piper Cherokees.

FLIGHT SIMULATOR

Overhead panel:
fuel control, **hydraulics**,
pressurization, lights,
air conditioning
Autopilot switches
Horizon
Airspeed
Altitude
Fire-warning light
Flight-management computer
Engine switches
G-YMMB
BG-KM

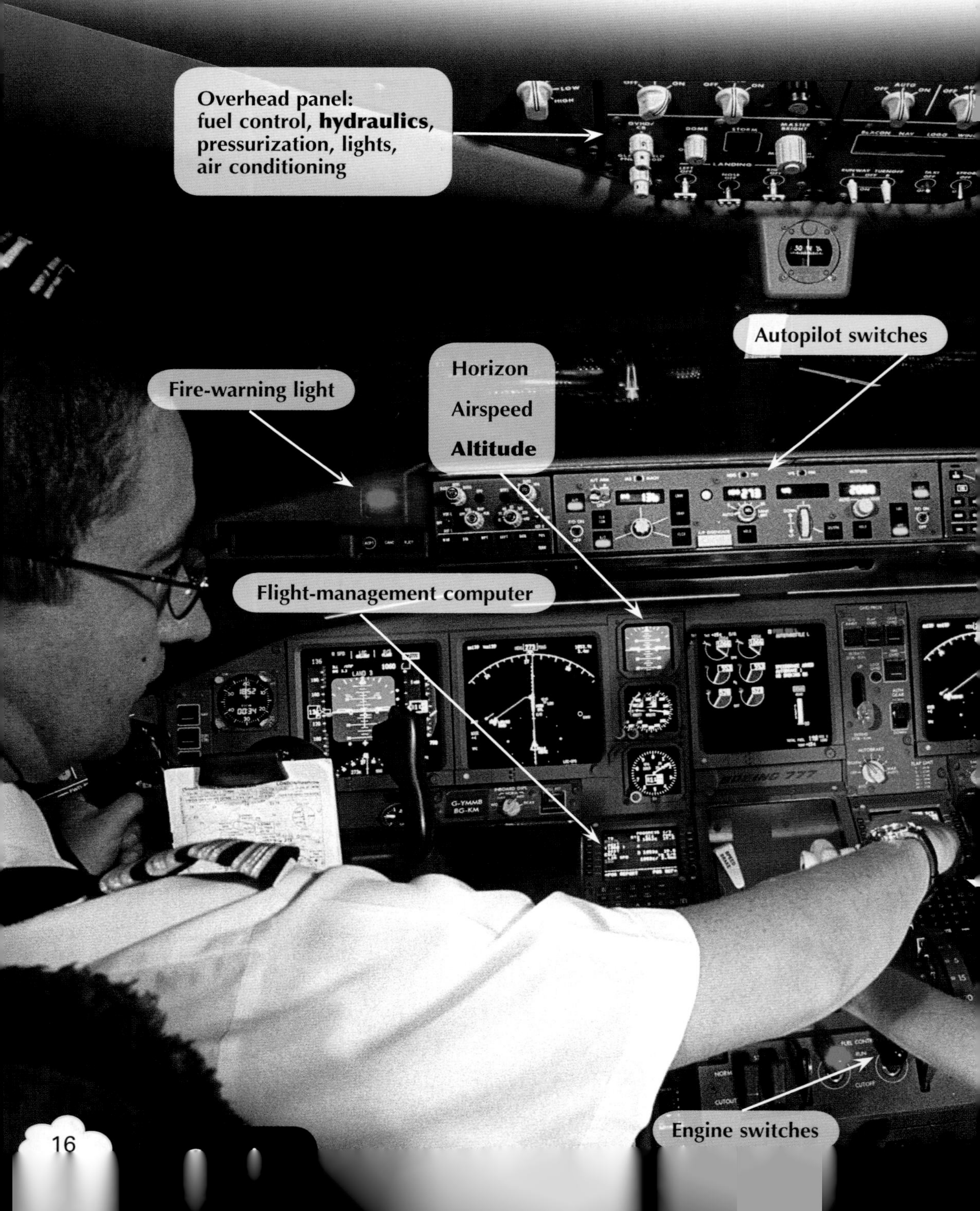

The inside of this flight simulator is a copy of the cockpit of a real Boeing 777. A computer linked to the controls provides realistic graphics of the view from the windows. The simulator is mounted on hydraulic legs so that the pilot can sense movement and forces.

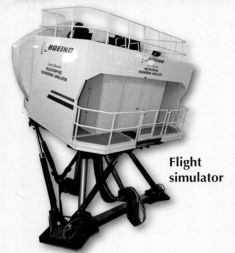

Flight simulator

Number 1 Engine on Fire!

Here the first officer is training with a captain in a flight simulator. She is practicing what to do in an emergency situation.

A fire–warning light indicates that the number 1 engine is on fire. The pilot continues to fly the aircraft and calls for the number 1 engine fire checklist. The copilot carries out the procedures on the checklist.

She starts by disconnecting the **auto–throttle** and closing down the number 1 thrust lever. She shuts off the fuel to number 1 engine and pulls the switch for the fire extinguisher on the number 1 engine. Using the stopwatch, if the fire is not out in 30 seconds, she operates the second fire extinguisher. As the pilots prepare for landing, the copilot declares a **mayday.** She warns the cabin crew to prepare for evacuation on landing. The pilots land the aircraft safely. The training session has been a success!

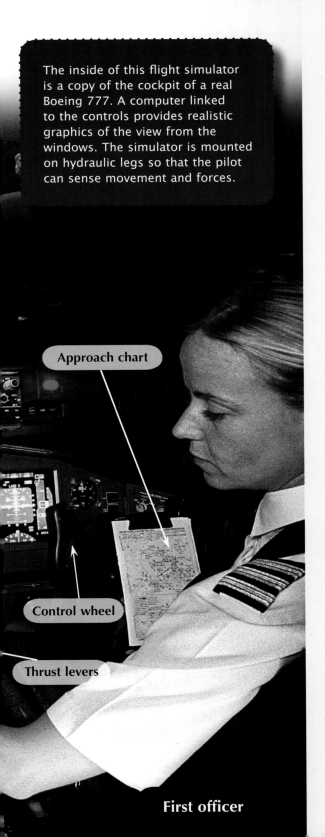

Approach chart

Control wheel

Thrust levers

First officer

TAKING OFF

Why do your ears pop after takeoff?

Airplanes fly at an altitude of about six and a half miles.
At that altitude, there is not enough oxygen in the air for human
respiration, so the airplane carries air around inside it.
If too much air is squeezed in, the airplane would bulge
like an overfilled balloon. To avoid this, the cabin air
is kept at a fairly low pressure. The air pressure
in the cabin is about the same as it would be at
the top of an 8,000-foot mountain. The pressure
is lowered after takeoff, causing little pockets
of air inside your ears to expand with a pop.
Your ears pop again when the pressure is raised
just before landing.

SHOCKER

Leaky airplane toilets
produce frozen chunks
of waste that sometimes
fall onto houses below.
Pilots call this
"blue ice."

Holding your nose and blowing
gently can help relieve the
pressure in your ears.

Where does the air inside the airplane come from?

Cabin air comes from the jet engines. It is cooled before going into the airplane. The air is completely replaced every five to ten minutes. The air inside the cabin is drier than in the driest deserts on the earth. Many people find it makes their eyes and throat scratchy and sore. The low pressure can also make you feel giddy and light-headed. One reason cabin air is so dry is to prevent corrosion of the metal parts. In the future, however, most airplanes will be built with composite materials, which are made by combining plastic with reinforcing material. The cabin air won't have to be kept so dry.

FLYING FACT

Dental work can leave small pockets of air inside your teeth. These pockets can expand on takeoff and give you a toothache. So don't fly for at least three days after going to the dentist.

?

I wasn't sure what cabin air was. Instead of worrying about it, I just kept reading. Reading on usually helps. Suddenly, it made sense. Cabin air is simply the air inside the cabin!

The wheels, or landing gear, fold back into compartments in the **fuselage** after takeoff.

IN THE AIR

How do jet engines work?

Jet engines suck air in, **compress** it, and heat it in a **combustion** chamber. The heated air is expanded in a **turbine**. The expanded air shoots out the back at a speed higher than the air around it. This pushes the airplane forward, creating thrust.

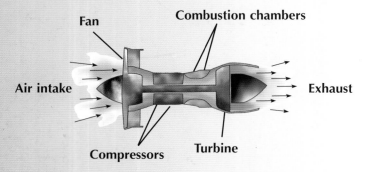

Fan

Combustion chambers

Air intake

Exhaust

Compressors

Turbine

Modern airliners all use a kind of jet engine called a turbofan. This engine sucks air in with a giant fan. Some of the air passes straight through, and some of it is heated in the combustion chambers.

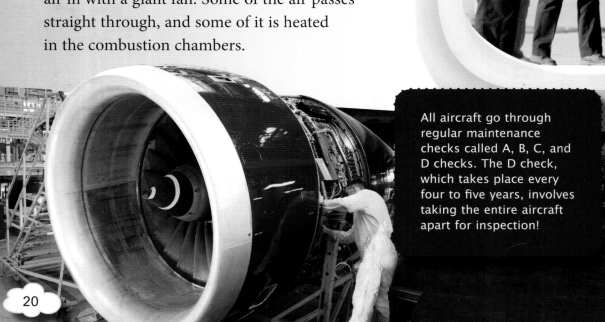

All aircraft go through regular maintenance checks called A, B, C, and D checks. The D check, which takes place every four to five years, involves taking the entire aircraft apart for inspection!

How does the airplane stay in the air?

To understand how an airplane flies, it helps to think of air as being like water flowing around the airplane. Airplane wings are curved so that air flows more quickly over the top of the wing than underneath. This reduces pressure on the top of the wing. The pressure difference between the top and bottom of the wing creates lift. The force of lift helps make airplanes fly.

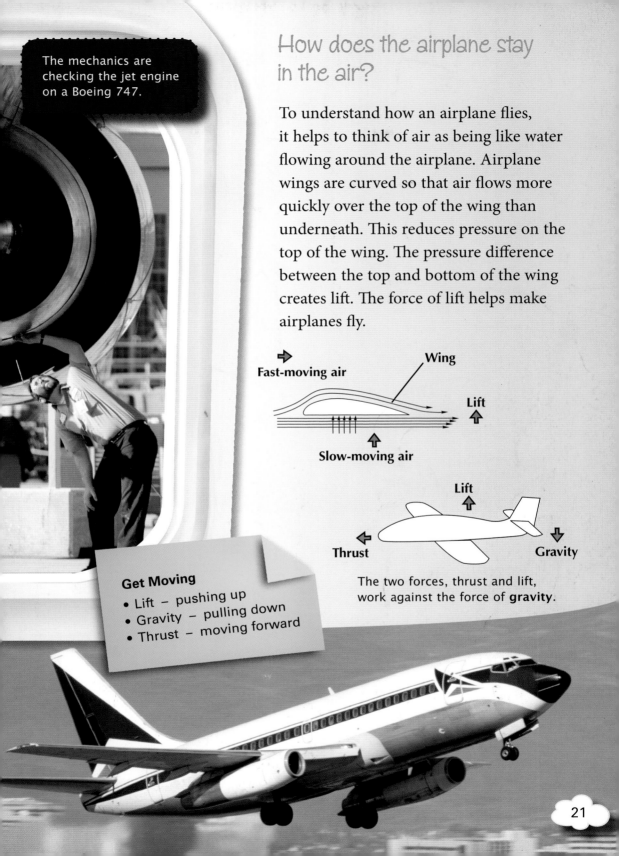

Fast-moving air

Wing

Lift

Slow-moving air

Lift

Thrust

Gravity

The two forces, thrust and lift, work against the force of **gravity**.

Get Moving
- Lift – pushing up
- Gravity – pulling down
- Thrust – moving forward

FINDING THE WAY

How do the pilots steer the plane?

The pilots fly the airplane with a control column that is similar to the joystick of a video game. It is made up of the column and the control wheel. Pushing or pulling on the column moves flaps on the tailplane which makes the nose rise or fall. Turning the control wheel moves flaps on the wings called ailerons, which make the plane roll. Foot pedals move the rudder (the hinged plate on the tail of the plane), which helps balance the aircraft. Ailerons and spoilers are used for turning the aircraft. Other flaps create lift or drag. On large airplanes, the control column sends electronic signals to motors under the wings that move the flaps.

Tailplane

Ailerons

Spoilers

So a control column is like a joystick. That makes it easier to understand. I've used a joystick many times while playing video games. Making connections makes reading easier.

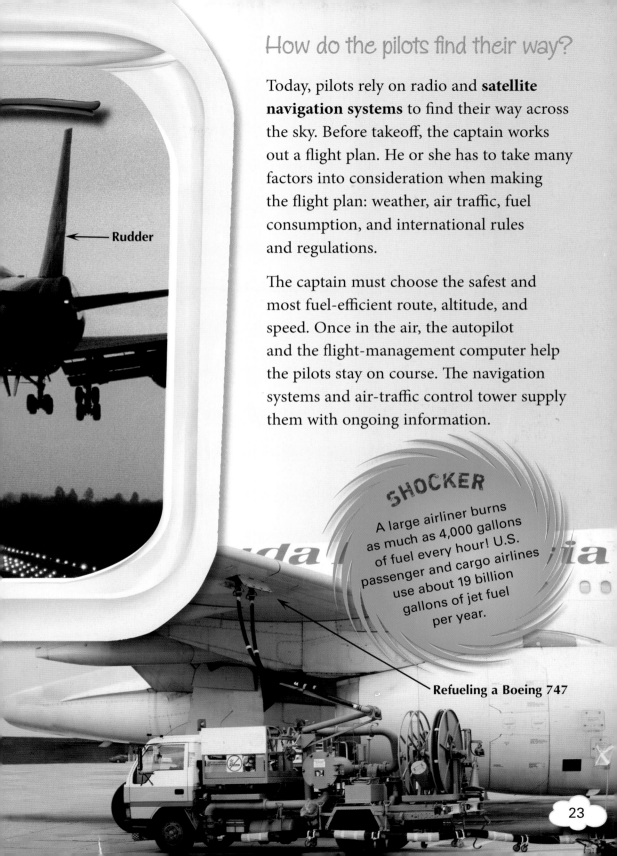

How do the pilots find their way?

Today, pilots rely on radio and **satellite navigation systems** to find their way across the sky. Before takeoff, the captain works out a flight plan. He or she has to take many factors into consideration when making the flight plan: weather, air traffic, fuel consumption, and international rules and regulations.

The captain must choose the safest and most fuel-efficient route, altitude, and speed. Once in the air, the autopilot and the flight-management computer help the pilots stay on course. The navigation systems and air-traffic control tower supply them with ongoing information.

Rudder

SHOCKER

A large airliner burns as much as 4,000 gallons of fuel every hour! U.S. passenger and cargo airlines use about 19 billion gallons of jet fuel per year.

Refueling a Boeing 747

SAFETY IN THE SKY

How safe is it to fly?

Airplanes are among the safest of all forms of transportation – they're far safer than cars! Skilled pilots, modern aircraft, and regular airplane maintenance have made flying safer than ever before.

In an emergency, an airliner is designed to be evacuated in 90 seconds in the dark, even if half the exits are blocked. Emergencies are rare, however. In recent years, there has been a drop in the number of air accidents, although more airplanes are flying than ever before.

Practicing for an Emergency

Flight crews and airport staff are highly trained to deal with emergencies. Flight crews practice evacuation procedures under extreme conditions. Airport fire crews use old airplanes to practice putting out airplane fires.

Why is the flight bumpy?

Warm air masses rise and cold ones sink. When an airplane passes through an area where warm and cold air meet, it can feel bumpy like a car going over a bumpy road. This is called turbulence. This kind of air movement usually cannot be seen and often happens unexpectedly. Turbulence can also be caused by **jet streams**, strong winds (particularly around mountains), and high and low pressure systems.

Most of the time, turbulence is not dangerous for airplanes. However, if the flight is very bumpy, people inside the plane can fall or bump into things and get injured. Since turbulence sometimes happens without warning, it's best to keep your seat belt on during the flight, just in case.

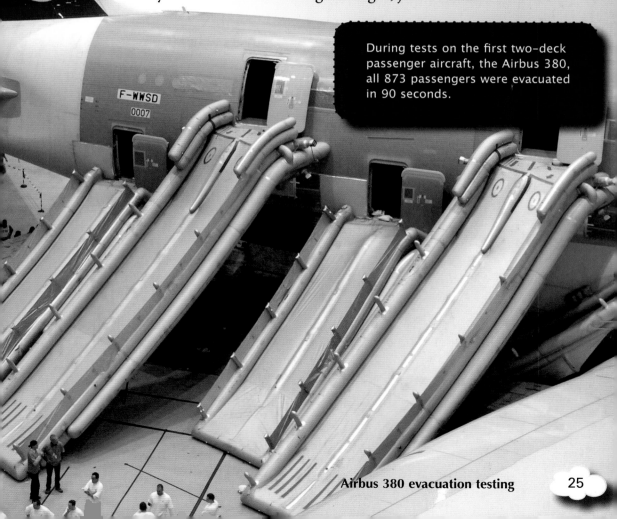

During tests on the first two-deck passenger aircraft, the Airbus 380, all 873 passengers were evacuated in 90 seconds.

F-WWSD
0007

Airbus 380 evacuation testing

What makes airplanes crash?

These days, there aren't many things that can make an airplane crash! There are many more safety systems in place than in the past. For example, many airplanes have automatic systems that prevent common pilot errors. Because ice on the wings can cause airplanes to lose lift, many airplanes now have heaters in the wings to melt ice. Ground crews also use antifreeze and steam to remove ice from airplanes.

Since **bird strike** is a hazard near airports, modern engines are built to withstand minor bird strikes. Airports also frighten away birds using noises, trained falcons, or dogs. Modern airplanes are also built so that lightning passes harmlessly across the outside of the airplane. The electronics on the airplane are shielded from the electrical current.

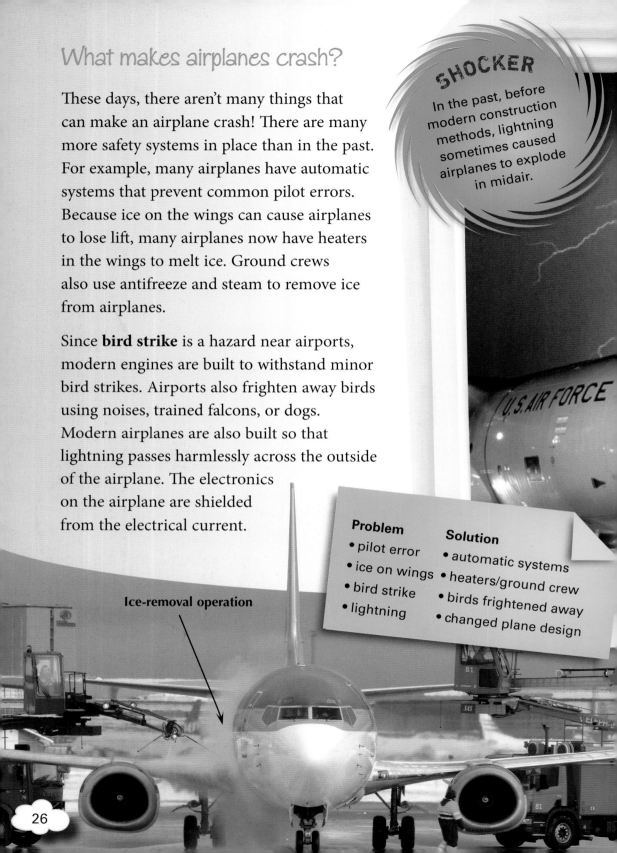

SHOCKER

In the past, before modern construction methods, lightning sometimes caused airplanes to explode in midair.

U.S. AIR FORCE

Ice-removal operation

Problem	Solution
• pilot error	• automatic systems
• ice on wings	• heaters/ground crew
• bird strike	• birds frightened away
• lightning	• changed plane design

What happens if a door opens in midair?

It is almost impossible for a modern airliner door to open in midflight. The reason is simple: the door is larger than the door frame. During flight, the air pressure inside the cabin is higher than outside. The cabin door is held in place like a plug. When the airplane lands, the air pressure inside and outside the airplane equalizes. It is then possible to swing the door inward to open it.

What is a black box?

A black box is a small device built into an airplane. It records all important data about the plane's performance. It usually has two parts: the flight data recorder and the cockpit voice recorder. This information is used for improving air safety and for explaining air accidents. Black boxes aren't black at all! They are usually painted bright orange to make them easier to find.

A typical airliner is struck by lightning twice a year.

This black box was retrieved after an air accident. The data it stored helped investigators figure out what happened.

27

LUCKY ESCAPES

Jungle Drop

On December 24, 1971, a German teenager, Juliane Koepcke, was on a flight from Lima, Peru. Her plane was struck by lightning and blew apart. The next thing Juliane knew, she was flying through the air, still strapped in her seat. She fell more than two miles, landing in some trees in the Amazon rain forest. When she came to, she was still in her airplane seat. She had some injuries, but was able to walk. Luckily, her scientist parents had taught her a great deal about surviving in the jungle. Juliane walked for nine days until she found help. She was the sole survivor of the crash. Her story amazed people around the world.

The words *came to* mean "to regain consciousness." There are many expressions that begin this way: *came to light*, *came to grips*, *came to pass*, *came to one's senses*, and so on.

Cloud of
volcanic ash

Deadly Cloud

"Ladies and gentlemen, this is your captain speaking. We have a problem. All four engines have stopped ..."

On June 24, 1982, a British Airways jet flew through a cloud of ash from Galunggung Volcano, on the island of Java in Indonesia. The volcano had been erupting for weeks. The ash clogged up the plane's engines. As the plane went into a steep dive, the crew prepared for an emergency landing in the ocean.

Suddenly, one engine after another roared back to life. The fresh air below the cloud had flushed out the ash. Luckily, the plane was able to land safely on three engines at Jakarta Airport, in Indonesia.

SHOCKER
Flight attendant Vesna Vulovic of Serbia survived a 33,000-foot fall onto snow-covered mountains when her plane was blown up by terrorists in 1972.

CARGO CARRIERS

What kinds of planes carry cargo?

Most passenger airplanes carry some freight. However, many airlines also have special cargo aircraft. These are planes that are built specially to carry cargo. These planes, such as the Boeing 747 freighter, look like passenger planes, except that they have no windows (other than in the cockpit, of course). Some cargo planes load freight through a door under the tail. Others flip open the nose of the plane. Boeing has developed a new cargo plane that swings the whole rear end of the fuselage open to load freight! It is called the Dreamlifter.

There are also cargo planes that look very different from passenger planes. They have very wide, fat bodies; high wings and tail; and a lot more wheels. Today, these kinds of cargo planes are used mainly by the military.

Cargo planes transport all kinds of things, including perishable fruit, huge trucks, and live animals! More than 85 horses can fit on a 747 cargo plane. In the past, horses were loaded into the plane and then stalls were built around them. Today, horses are usually loaded into special air stables, which are then lifted into the cargo hold. Specially trained crew fly with animals to take care of them during the flight.

The Dreamlifter was specially designed to transport parts for the new Boeing passenger airplane, the Dreamliner.

Nose flipped open

This cargo plane is transporting a part of the International Space Station from Italy, where it was built, to the Kennedy Space Center.

In the early days of airlines, flying was only for the wealthy few. Now, with lower airfares, more people are flying than ever before. This has been good for tourism and trade. However, it has been bad for the environment. Airliners burn large amounts of fuel and contribute to climate change. Also, as airports expand to meet demand, more homes suffer from round-the-clock jet noise, pollution, and traffic.

WHAT DO YOU THINK?

Should we avoid flying, for the sake of the environment, and use other forms of transportation instead?

PRO

I think that flying is here to stay! Almost every kind of transportation produces emissions. Besides, flying is sometimes the only way to get to faraway places. Cheap flights have made it possible for more families and friends to stay in touch.

Some people think we should fly less, in order to protect the environment. Others point out that aircraft exhaust makes up only a small part of overall **emissions**. Many people believe that the answer is carbon credits. Buying a carbon credit gives a person or business the right to emit one metric ton of carbon dioxide. The idea is to reduce emissions by giving them a monetary value that can be bought and sold.

CON

I think we should fly less. Most flights are for nonessential reasons, such as overseas vacations. We can reduce the amount we fly by taking vacations closer to home. We should also avoid buying food that has been flown around the world.

GLOSSARY

altitude (*AL ti tood*) the height of something above the ground

auto-throttle part of the autopilot that moves the thrust levers in response to speed requirements

avionics (*ay vee ON iks*) electronic instrumentation and control equipment used in airplanes

bird strike a collision between a bird and the engine of an airplane

combustion (*kuhm BUSS chuhn*) the process of catching fire and burning

compress (*cum PRESS*) to press or squeeze something so that it will fit into a small space

consumption (*kuhn SUHMP shuhn*) the process of using up a product

emission a substance released into the air

gravity the force that pulls objects toward the surface of the earth

hydraulic (*hye DRAW lik*) operated on power created when liquid is forced under pressure through pipes

inorganic (*in or GAN ik*) made up of matter other than plant or animal matter

jet stream a very strong current of wind, usually about eight miles above the earth's surface

mayday a word used all over the world to ask for help or rescue. It comes from "M'aidez", which is French for "Help me!"

organic made up of substances that come from living things

respiration the process in humans and animals of taking in oxygen and sending out carbon dioxide

satellite navigation system a navigation system that determines location based on signals received from a satellite

simulator (*SIM you lay tur*) a machine that allows you to experience what it is like to fly a plane by using computer technology, film, and mechanical movement

turbine (*TUR bine*) an engine driven by water, steam, or gas passing through the blades of a wheel and making it revolve

Turbine

FIND OUT MORE

BOOKS

Hopkins, Ellen. *Air Devils: Sky Racers, Sky Divers, and Stunt Pilots.* Perfection Learning, 2000.

Murray, Jennifer. *Flight and Fancy: The Airline Industry.* Scholastic Inc., 2008.

Oxlade, Chris. *Airplanes: Uncovering Technology.* Firefly Books, 2006.

Platt, Richard. *Flight.* DK Publishing, 2006.

Rinard, Judith E. *Book of Flight: The Smithsonian National Air and Space Museum.* Firefly Books, 2007.

Sandler, Martin W. *Flying Over the U.S.A.: Airplanes in American Life.* Oxford University Press, U.S.A., 2004.

WEB SITES

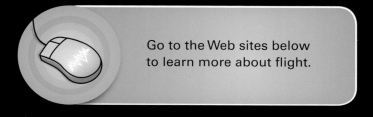

Go to the Web sites below to learn more about flight.

www.planemath.com/activities/pmenterprises/forces/forces1.html

www.howstuffworks.com/airplane.htm

www.nasm.si.edu/exhibitions/gal100/gal100.html

http://sln.fi.edu/flights/own2/forces.html

http://library.thinkquest.org/C004036F/sitemap.html

INDEX

air pressure	18–19, 25, 27
air-traffic control	12–13, 23
black box	27
cargo	10, 23, 30–31
computers	10–12, 14, 16–17, 23
dogs	8, 10, 26
emergencies	15–17, 24–25, 28–29
engines	16–21, 26, 29
flight simulators	15–17
fuel	13–14,
jet streams	
lightning	
luggage	
maintenance	
pilots	13–
turbulence	
X-rays	

ABOUT THE AUTHOR

Peter Rees lives in a seaside town in Wales where he writes and edits books for young people. He loves to travel by air, rail, and sea. However, as he owns neither an airplane, a train nor a ship, he usually gets around on a bicycle!